*Dedicated to the memory of
my mother, Rockymarie Weaver,
and my father, Edward J. Cullinane.
Life was hard for each of us.
I forgive you. I miss you.*

ALMOST TWELVE

Uncovering My Journey Through Grief

Maeve A. Cullinane

Almost Twelve: Uncovering My Journey Through Grief
Maeve A. Cullinane

Published by Synergy Publishing Group, Belmont, NC
Formatting and design by Melisa Graham

Softcover, May 2026, ISBN 978-1-960892-72-0
Ebook, May 2026, ISBN 978-1-960892-73-7

To everything (turn, turn, turn)
There is a season (turn, turn, turn)
And a time to every purpose under heaven
—Pete Seeger

A Time to Die

Many people have died in my life. For as long as I can remember, death has been part of my life's story, on the list with more commonplace events like moving to a new house or graduating from high school. Death is not as joyful for sure, but simply an ever-present feature in my life journey. I had to learn that this is not true for everyone.

For me, each new death reverberates with echoes of past losses. On the anniversaries and birthdays of the people who have died, I am sent into a reverie of reflection. Sometimes, I find myself uplifted by these touchstone days; I'm contemplative and full of love, receiving perspective on the wonderful relationships and blessings in my life. At other times, I am depressed, debilitated, pulled into gray holes I thought I had climbed out of. There is a litany of losses, and a new one to add.

To function, I developed an ability to be matter-of-fact about my experiences. If asked, I simply list the deaths in my life the way people may tick off items to be remembered each day—keys, phone, earbuds, reading glasses, water bottle, umbrella. I have accustomed myself to putting it out there quickly, maybe bluntly, casually even. I cannot avoid the fact that there have been deaths in my life, that they are part of me, but I also know that others find it difficult to take in.

My brother, Mark. My "grandfather," Kinsey. My dad. My mom, Rocky. The big deaths come up first, the people who were very important. Everyone is, of course, important, and every life matters, but there are those who have been most important, in their lives and in their deaths. These are the loved ones I wailed over, and who come back to me the heaviest.

As I push toward the last decades of my life, it's understandable that grief and loss come more often. Longtime friends are dying, and I realize that my friends, who didn't grow up like I did, are entering this world of mourning for the first time. I wonder what I can share about grief.

The very first person who died while I was living was my paternal grandmother, Margaret Kenny Cullinane, who lived in Boston. She died when I was a little girl, perhaps in kindergarten, too young to remember the half-dozen or so visits we must have taken to her home in Dorchester. I don't remember her. She was old, died naturally, and by all accounts had a fine life. There is one iconic story of her life, a story of immigration from Ireland when she was only thirteen, leaving Galway on a boat to America with only what she could carry, including thread, bobbins, and pins in her undergarments in order to make lace like generations of women before her. I was too young to go to the funeral, so I didn't meet my uncles, or her daughter, who probably brought her food on Sundays or took her to Mass. I stayed at my other grammy's house and ate her pie.

That other grammy lived a long life and is much later on in the chronological list of deaths. She died an old woman too, surviving her husband by over a decade. Her funeral filled the town church with her grown daughters and their families, many friends, and other relatives. She had worked as a volunteer in the church thrift shop and moved to the new senior housing village when it opened. When you age and all your friends are aging with you, funerals become as much a part of life as taking a trip or reading a book. It's what happens. In middle age, even the death of grandparents and parents is sad, but not shocking. By the time folks are retired, wrinkled, or senile, having lived long, hopefully good lives, mourning their deaths includes a sense of bringing the Circle of Life round right.

I don't mean these losses are inconsequential. My mother's death at age eighty-two was rough; she declined mentally over two years with Lewy body dementia, needing increased caregiving and support. After she died, I spent the next couple of years feeling unmoored, now an orphan in the world. I can never replace her, but part of my healing has been rooted in the understanding that her life would never go on forever. She had beaten cancer once. She had survived the loss of her son and a divorce, and reinvented herself. Even without believing in heaven, she left this world for an easier place.

These classic verses shared with me at my mother's death gave me solace: "To everything there is a season, and a time to every purpose under heaven: a time to be born, and a time to die …" (Ecclesiastes 3:1–2 KJV). Those same verses have failed me with other deaths, the ones that came unexpectedly and untimely. Sudden deaths are not worse or harder, but the weight and longevity of those losses are different, with less rhythm to the pain and grieving.

In my thirty-third year, somewhere in the middle of deaths I've experienced, I lost a baby at thirteen weeks. I didn't lose a person I loved, nor even a person really. I lost a wonderful, half-baked, but much-anticipated idea of a second child. After receiving the news of my miscarriage, post-ultrasound, I wept uncontrollably in a hospital gown, alone in a dressing room cubicle. I wept for the baby my family would never meet, and for the days my baby and I would never spend together. And I wept for each of the losses that had come before, each death that had taken from me imagined yet unlived experiences, dreams that could not come true. I wept hard. Loss is loss, and grief flooded me, even for this smallest of deaths.

The biggest death on my list would have to be my brother's. He was twenty, and I was almost twelve.

1

My sixth-grade class was finishing up rehearsing *Julius Caesar*. The performance was still a couple of weeks off, but this was the last time using scripts. "Off book tomorrow," Miss Godwin reminded us. I tried to say my lines without looking at the stapled sheaf of pages our teacher had given us. The play was the culminating activity of our Ancient Greece unit. Next week we would make headpieces in art class and learn to wrap togas—but first, we had to know all our lines.

"I have a lot more memorizing to do tonight," whispered Laura. I should do a little too, but I actually felt pretty confident about my lines. I was more concerned about remembering my cues.

"I'm going to study mine tonight too," I reassured her. After all, I'd rather be over-prepared. I was learning this about myself. I was going to junior high next year, and it was important to know how we learned best.

The play was part of social studies, my favorite class. We hardly ever just sat in our desks with this new unit, MACOS, or Man: A Course of Study. Miss Godwin informed us it was an innovative way of teaching about history and science and society. She had us role-playing, making dioramas, and playing games. It was a lot of

fun, especially because we worked in small groups,
and that meant more time with Mary Ann and Laura.
We had done other neat projects, but this play was
the best. I wished we could do social studies all day
long. I had learned that social studies was one of my
favorite subjects.

Forty-five minutes later, Miss Godwin released us.
Math class was next, the last class of every day. I stopped
at the long, gray metal lockers outside the art room to
stash my script. Mary Ann followed. She and I were
best friends. I had known most of the kids in my grade
since kindergarten, having had different best friends
over the years. Mary Ann had parakeets in her dining
room, several brothers, and a big house in the woods.
She liked coming over to my house or hanging out in the
library with us after school. We both thought math was
a lot more boring than social studies, except that Mr.
McManus was super nice. He had been a teacher for a
long time and told us about many of his former students
and his family.

Mr. McManus liked to tell stories, so we often
tried to get him sidetracked from the worksheets on
multiplying fractions. Asking him about his fishing
trips was foolproof. For Christmas, a few of us had gone
in together and bought him a Tupperware toolbox to
hold his flies and lures. It was bright blue and made of
indestructible, waterproof plastic. We figured, even if he
had another fishing box, he'd need one like this. Several
mothers sold Tupperware at parties in their homes, so it
was easy to find someone to order from. It was my first

Christmas buying secret presents. I had bought my mom
a set of stacking avocado and gold mixing bowls. Mary
Ann bought her mom a stacking set of measuring cups.
We heard that next year, in junior high, we would get to
take home economics and actually cook on a stove and
make desserts at school. I couldn't wait! Mr. McManus
reminded us that we would need to know a lot about
fractions if we were going to be good cooks.

Halfway into math, the principal appeared at our
door and handed a note to Mr. McManus. They both
looked up at me as the principal left the room. Then the
lesson continued. I wondered what that was about. Mr.
McManus turned to the board and droned on about
common denominators. Fifteen more minutes until the
end of the day. He gave us our homework assignment
and a reminder that the chapter test would be on
Thursday, followed by Memorial Day weekend. The bell
rang, and we all sprang into action.

"Maeve, can I see you for a minute?" Mr. McManus
called to me. I glanced at Mary Ann, and she shrugged
her shoulders. She tried to slow down her steps as she
walked out the door.

"Yes. You need me?"

"Yes, I have a note saying you are supposed to go to
the Clymers' house after school. Family friends?" he
asked, looking hopeful.

"Oh. Yup. Okay." I felt confused, which made me
unsure how to answer him.

"You are to pick up your sister from her classroom
and walk straight there. You know the way? They live at

the west edge of the schoolyard, don't they? Lily Lane?"
He was speaking much faster than usual, and sounded
uncharacteristically nervous. I liked him better when
his sentences weren't questions.

"We have gone there before from school. Sometimes.
I thought I was taking the bus home …"

"Well, the note says your mom called and wants you
and your sister to go to the Clymers.'" He showed me
the note, and that's all it said. I had several questions
forming in my head, but it seemed obvious that Mr.
McManus would not have the answers. He looked as
befuddled as I felt.

"Okay. Thank you. Can I go get Deirdre now?"

"Yes. Good idea … see you tomorrow."

Dinner with the Clymers was quiet but delicious. They
were an older couple, friends of my parents, whose
small stucco house was a stone's throw from the school.
Mr. Clymer had a white goatee and really kind eyes.
His skin was very wrinkled, and he was retired. It never
occurred to me to ask what he had retired from. He
didn't talk much, but when he asked me about my day,
he listened intently to my answers. Mrs. Clymer was
a children's author. My mom was the town's children's
librarian, so they were very good friends. Mrs. Clymer
read at the library sometimes and once showed us
the drafts of a new book she was working on. She had
even dedicated a book each to my sister and me. We
loved the Clymers like grandparents, but we had never

spent a night at their house before, or visited without my parents.

The four of us ate dinner around their trestle table with ladder-back chairs that rose high above our heads. The wicker seats were old and soft, the table without shine but golden brown. Deirdre and I were each served a full plate of food: spaghetti with one meatball drenched in a chunky red sauce, two slices of buttery garlic bread with green flecks on it, and a handful of green beans. I looked at my little sister as she looked at the food. She never ate anything green or chunky, but she did like bread and plain spaghetti noodles. I hoped she would simply do her best and eat around the things she detested. I thanked Mrs. Clymer profusely for making us dinner, and she insisted I call her Eleanor. She was so kind, and I loved being with her, but I was still unsure why we were there. In a rush, I asked her if she knew where my parents were.

"Oh, New Hampshire. Didn't they tell you at school? I assumed you were told," she replied earnestly.

New Hampshire had been one place I thought they could be. That's where my big brother lived. I couldn't remember now whether Mr. McManus had told me that, or if Deirdre had, or if I should have known. Eleanor sounded a little mad at my school, and I didn't want her to be.

"They told me. I just forgot," I quickly responded. She looked at me with great concern, and that made me think I should be concerned. This had been an afternoon of adult expressions that puzzled me. "Well, what I meant was … why are they in New Hampshire?"

For the first time in my life, a grown-up looked at me with pity. Pity is not something I was familiar with, but I became very familiar with it over the coming years.

Eleanor took a breath and then simply explained that my parents had to go to New Hampshire suddenly, and they weren't sure how late they'd be getting back. They thought it would be best for us to sleep there at the Clymers' house. They would explain more when they came home. I asked if they were seeing Mark in New Hampshire, but they didn't answer the question.

"That's all I know, honey. Now let's go make up a bed for you two. Do you mind sleeping in the big double bed under the eaves? It'll be an adventure!" I felt like I was on an adventure, so maybe the eaves would make it more fun.

And it sure was, although probably not the way Eleanor wanted. After we set up our bed, Eleanor read to us from her book *The Trolley Car Family,* one of our favorites. Then she said good night and went downstairs. Deirdre and I looked at each other.

"Are you tired?" I asked.

"No," she answered. "Why are we here?" she asked. My little sister was very smart, very blunt, and very stubborn.

I shrugged my shoulders. "We'll find out in the morning." Then I started telling her knock-knock jokes, and she told me some. I asked, "What is black and white and red all over?" and we came up with six different hilarious and gross answers. "A zebra in a blender!" Then we shared as many dead baby jokes as we could remember. "What's worse than a truckload of dead babies? Two truckloads!"

We got the major giggles. Eleanor popped her head in and suggested we had better turn out the light and try to sleep. As she left, I stood up on the squeaky spring mattress and tried to reach the string pull on the overhead light. Squeak, squeak. Deirdre joined me, and we bounced hand in hand, as if we were on a trampoline. Our beds at home were not nearly as springy as this ancient contraption. It truly had metal springs! We got so boisterous that Eleanor returned to tell us to calm down. She turned off the light herself this time and tucked us in. Beneath the sheets, we tunneled and made crazy faces to bring smiles to each other. We held our breath and tried not to make a sound—until one of us got the hiccups and that made us giggle. We had to come up for air! Losing control, we laughed hard again. Eleanor returned and told us a bit more sternly to quiet down. It went on like that until she said she would have to separate us if we didn't go to sleep. It was almost midnight, and we were exhausted. We fell asleep holding on to each other, crosswise, on the bed.

I woke up with a sunbeam across my face. Looking out the small dormer window, I noted that the sun was fairly high in the sky. I opened my eyes fully and couldn't quite place where I was. A sparrow sat on a birch branch. My window at home looked out at the neighbor's roof and then down to our gravel driveway. Where was this birch tree? I turned my head and saw my sister in bed with me. I looked up at the dormer ceiling and down at the wide pine boards. This old Cape house was nothing like our contemporary Colonial. The bookcase beside the bed was filled with multiple copies of Eleanor Clymer's books. Oh right. The Clymers' house. I shoved Deirdre with my foot.

"I think we are missing school," I said. It had to be almost 10 a.m. I could hear the noises of people moving around downstairs. Deirdre sat up and rubbed her eyes. I looked away from her and watched the sparrow until it flew away. I decided I'd better go find out when we were going home.

2

My brother was dead. My parents didn't say it that way, but that's what it came down to. I wish they had said those words, because the ones they started with confused me. I wasn't sure I had heard them right. Their words cycled over and over in my mind, like gears trying to catch but not engaging. At first, it seemed possible that I had misunderstood. If my brother was gone or passed away, couldn't that mean he was lost or on some faraway trip? Their words left open that possibility. Besides, my family frequently teased me for missing the point of jokes and innuendo.

In hindsight, I wondered if they had simply said those four words, "your brother is dead," maybe it would have been easier. Maybe. Maybe not. I certainly didn't want to hear them. My brother, Mark, was eight years older than me, tall and long-haired and special, and very much alive to me. It was 1973, and he lived at a commune in New Hampshire. He baked bread for the bakery, sang Sanskrit chants like monks, and wore wool ponchos through the winter. I loved everything about him, especially when he called me "miz frutz" and looked right into my eyes when I told him stuff. How could he not be alive? He was all about life and living. It was

difficult to imagine the *dead* part. I kept thinking through
what my parents had told us—something about a fire, an
accident, a tragedy, a truck, gasoline, a loss to his friends,
how much he loved us … they kept talking and talking,
or rather, my mom kept talking and talking. My dad held
her hand at first, and then just sat quietly with his head
bowed. She never said that he was dead or that he'd been
killed. Had she? I wasn't sure. I didn't want to be sure.

The next night, I lay in my own bed in my own room,
which was first Mark's when he was in high school.
He had painted one wall fire-engine red, but I asked
to repaint it yellow. My dad said it would be too hard
priming that dark a color in order to make it yellow. I
acquiesced and moved the bunk bed against that wall
to cover up most of the red. But now, when I lay in
bed, the red wall burned beside me. Mark was never
coming back into this room. I squeezed my eyes tightly
together, wishing to take back the past twenty-four
hours. We should have been better guests at the Clymers.'
We shouldn't have bounced on their antique bed. My
eyes flooded, and I squeezed them tight. I squeezed and
wished. I imagined the first star of the night was outside
my window. Wish I may, wish I might. I squeezed my
eyes shut and wished hard. I just wanted my brother
back. For many nights I tried that, squeezing and wishing.
It never worked. The tragedy that colored the rest of my
entire life was always there, and I could never squeeze
away from it.

We didn't go to school that day, nor the next, nor
for several more. My dad didn't drive his station wagon

to work in the morning. He shut himself in the den.
My mom was on the phone a lot. Relatives started
appearing, and casseroles too. There was so much food
in our house, and extra people, but I don't remember
sitting down to an evening dinner on any of those
first nights. And I could sleep in as late as I wanted
every morning. My mom never came to wake me up
anymore. Deirdre wore pajamas all day long, even
outside on the swing set. No one told her to get dressed
until I did.

A couple of days in, the Clymers came over. We
hadn't seen them since our overnight stay. When I
answered the door, Eleanor drew me close to her and
hugged my whole back and head.

"I'm so sorry," she said.

"That's okay!" I said chirpily. I thought she was
apologizing because she had been so stern to us that
night. She looked at me oddly and bent to kiss my
cheek, sighing the words "oh, honey" into my ear. That's
when I realized she meant she was sorry about Mark
being dead, and I felt stupid. "Thank you," I mumbled.

Mr. Clymer suggested we take my dog, Sammy, for a
walk. With Deirdre too.

"Okay," I shrugged.

"No, thanks," my sister said.

"Um, you better just come anyway," he said. Deirdre
shrugged her shoulders and followed.

I'd never gone on a walk with Mr. Clymer before. He
said I could call him Kinsey, but it felt uncomfortable,
so mostly I just smiled and didn't use a name. We

went as far as the Triangle, where three streets in our neighborhood came together and left a green patch with a beech tree. It was the meeting place for all games of kick the can. Several kids younger than I were splitting up for teams. As we got nearer, they all stopped talking and stood still. Kinsey said we should go back the other way, so we turned around and continued past my house and partway up the road and into the woods. I loved those woods, and I could tell Kinsey did too. He was looking up at the trees, and his shoulders relaxed. It seemed like a long time since I had walked there, which was strange because I went into the woods any chance I could get. It felt odd to be there with a grown-up, and I had never walked Sammy, my Pekingese, into the woods! The steep road narrowed to a dirt path, strewn with fallen branches. Sammy was low to the ground, and his fur stuck on leaves and twigs. His little legs strained up the steep hill. I saw Deirdre furtively watching the trees and shadows. She looked a little spooked. It suddenly didn't seem like a good idea to be there anymore.

"I think Sammy is getting tired," I said, hoping it sounded polite and not panicky.

"Alright then. Let's bring him home." We turned around and descended to the paved road of our neighborhood.

As we opened the door to my house, I could hear my mom's voice, a little more high-pitched than usual.

"That will be fine. Ed? Right?"

"Fine." My dad's voice was lower and quieter. "Thank you, Eleanor."

"Consider it done. We will see you at the meetinghouse on Saturday, about half an hour before. You don't need to do anything more."

And that is how I learned we were having Mark's memorial service at the Clymers' Quaker meetinghouse. There had been several hushed conversations in the previous days, comments I had tried to piece together, some overheard from my mom's phone calls. Now I knew we would not have the Irish wake or the Catholic Mass or the graveside funeral, which were the traditional options relatives had discussed. For some reason, the decision seemed fraught with complication. I didn't understand why, but I figured it made sense for my hippie brother, my agnostic mother, and my lapsed Catholic father to do something different like this. I had never been to a Quaker meeting, though, so I hoped someone would tell me what to do.

That same day, my best friend, Mary Ann, sent me a sympathy card with a picture of a girl in a flowing white dress standing against an orange sunset with script lettering. The card said, "Sometimes when one person is missing, the whole world suddenly seems depopulated." I cried with my whole soul when I read it.

Receiving a sympathy card addressed to me felt very grown-up, and Mary Ann seemed very grown-up for sending it. However, when I actually read it while sitting under the lilac bush beside our house, I was overwhelmed. I cried so hard, barely making a sound. I blew my nose and read it for a second time. Then I felt empty, but I knew that wasn't actually a feeling. It was a lack of feeling, a helpless non-feeling. I sat there, under the branches, not feeling and not thinking. Except I *do* remember hoping that no one else would send me another sympathy card.

The next afternoon, while aunts and neighbors were in the kitchen and living room downstairs, Deirdre and I sat upstairs reading in her bedroom. Her room had been our shared room for most of our lives. We retreated there, comforted by its walls, and away from my brother's red wall. I don't remember talking much, but I do remember being next to one another most of every day. My dad called for us.

"Girls, come on downstairs." We shot each other a look and put down our books. His voice sounded foreign calling out that familiar phrase. We heard his footsteps receding on the stair treads. We slowly marched out of the bedroom. Looking down the stairs, we saw Mom and Dad in the front hall, looking up at us expectantly.

"We want you to come on an errand with us," my mom said matter-of-factly. They were both dressed in regular clothes, not fancy and not pajamas. They weren't crying. I looked at Deirdre, and she shrugged her shoulders. We hadn't gone anywhere or done anything with them since the day they came back. My mom hugged me anytime she saw me, but otherwise drifted through the house. We hadn't sat at the dinner table, had bedtime stories, or checked on the garden.

The last time I remember sitting with them was on the couch when they told us about losing Mark.

The car ride was long and quiet. We filled up the gas tank shortly after leaving the house and drove out of town, but not on any usual route I recognized. Not toward the grocery store or the skating rink, or the shops in Mt. Kisco. I wasn't sure where we were going. Mom put on the radio, and Dad unrolled the window. I tried to convince myself that it was a weekend drive to see the countryside, and I wondered if we might go to Friendly's for ice cream. I whispered the idea to Deirdre, and she nodded in agreement. I gestured with my finger to say nothing. A few miles later, on a long stretch of road with no houses or other cars, my dad pulled our car way over onto the shoulder. He and Mom looked at each other and turned around to face us over the bench seat.

"Girls, we wanted to talk to you about something you might hear people saying about Mark," explained my mother in her most patient and librarian-sounding voice.

This felt an awful lot like the sit-down conversation they'd had with us a week ago, the one that had left me sad, the one that had changed everything. I really did not want to feel any more pain, but I knew there was nothing I could do about it. I held my sister's hand. My mother nodded to my father to begin.

"Girls," he said, taking a deep breath before launching into the speech. "There was a reporter from the newspaper who printed an obituary that is not what your mother and I wrote. He spoke to some people up in New Hampshire, on his own, and has written that Mark, uh, com—well, that his death was not an accident, that he meant it." And then my dad ran out of words. He looked away from us, out the driver's window. I struggled to understand, to even remember what my dad had just said.

My mom filled the silence with a rush of words. "We know our Marky, and we know how much he loved us and loved … everything. He would not have done that. The fire was a terrible accident, and those gas cans were out there where he was working on that truck … there are simply things we cannot know. We won't know. But we *do* know … how hard this is … for you, our sweet girls. And how much Mark loved both of you. We just wanted to be sure you knew that and not to … not to worry, don't worry about what people say happened."

My dad had turned away to look straight ahead out the windshield. He gripped the steering wheel with his big hands and dropped his head. My mom touched his arm. He mumbled something that might have been "he loved us" or maybe "we loved him." My mom pursed her lips and looked back at us. She inhaled tentatively and asked very seriously, "Can we answer any questions for you?"

I looked at her blankly. What? Questions? My brain was tripping over isolated phrases like "meant it" and "accident." "We know" and "we couldn't know." I saw my dad's heaving shoulders and silent crying. His tears dropped onto the new leather steering wheel cover he had bought on a whim that blazing hot day last summer. I closed my eyes.

"Anything?" my mom repeated.

I mumbled "no," and my sister mimicked me.

"We love you both." It felt like there was more she wanted to say, but my dad started up the car, and she faced frontward in her seat.

I looked out the passenger window at the strange field, and again wondered where we were. This was my first time here. I hoped my dad knew how to get home from here. That's when Deirdre piped up and said, "Mom? I do have one question."

"Yes, sweetie?" Mom replied quickly.

"Can we get ice cream at Friendly's?" My parents guffawed, surprise and relief welling up in them.

"Absolutely! Jim Dandies for everyone!" my dad exclaimed and wiped his nose with the back of his hand.

On Saturday, we parked beside the meetinghouse. It was really cool. Cool temperature-wise, as the building was in a shady dell, but the decor and structure were cool too. It was an ancient building of stone and wood. The central room was unadorned and nothing like my Catholic grandmother's stained glass church or the Presbyterian one my sister and I peeked into around the corner from our house. This Quaker building had wooden pews set in a square, no pulpit, and a low ceiling. For the memorial, floor pillows filled the center of the room. It was dim, cool, plain, and extraordinarily quiet.

My brother was only twenty when he died. He had graduated from high school two years before, and many friends from his high school days came to pay their respects. Friends from my school came with their parents, and I marvelled at how they all heard the news. The Clymers were there, and many adults I recognized from around town, my parents' community theater group, and our neighborhood, in addition to all the relatives. My dad's sister, Peggy, and her family came from Boston, and I'd only ever seen her a few times in my whole life. Dad had some brothers who didn't come; I couldn't even remember how many of them he had. Of course, my mom's family was there. Her four sisters had been around for several days, organizing the casseroles in the fridge and reading sympathy cards to my parents. Their spouses and some of their children had arrived last night.

The service itself was supposed to be mostly silent. That's how Quakers worship, "waiting for that of God" to come to them and possibly lead them "quaking" to share a message with those gathered. That's how Eleanor explained it to Deirdre and me that morning. A memorial meeting would have messages about the deceased and the meaning of loss or life or pertinent things like that. She told us we didn't have to do anything, just listen and hold what was being said. Once most people were settled, Kinsey stood up and spoke in the loudest voice I had ever heard from him.

"Thank you for coming and celebrating the life of Mark Edward Cullinane, in the manner of Friends." He explained the nature of the memorial service and then sat back down. Over the next forty-five minutes, several people spoke about my brother's wonderful spirit and how deeply he would be missed. No one said anything about how he died. No one actually said he was dead. Tissues appeared, and people handed them around as they cried. I definitely noticed the crying.

Crying was not something I had been very familiar with at the age of eleven, almost twelve. I had not cried myself very much up to that point in my life. Maybe when I skinned my knee or fell out of the crabapple tree, with tears that were easily cured with a Band-Aid or deep breaths. Crying had never shaken my whole body or left my face puffy, as it had this past week. I knew now that crying could simply come over you, starting in your heart and rolling through your ribcage, choking your breath, and pouring out your eyes. It wasn't attached to a feeling necessarily, and things that should have made me feel better, like when Deirdre crept into my bed at night, sometimes made me cry longer. She clung to me, and we both cried, wordlessly. When my aunt held me, seeing me after I read Mary Ann's card, she said to me, "That's a good girl," as I sobbed into her blouse. So I guess I was doing it right, but it sure felt terrible.

In the meetinghouse, especially on the floor of children and young people, there was a lot of crying going on, arms around each other, sniffling and snorting and hand holding. We heard a few more kind and somber messages, and then the service was over. I blew my nose and walked out into the yard. I don't remember anything else from the rest of the afternoon.

3

The day after the service, things seemed to be wrapping up. The relatives were starting to leave. Friends were fussing over my parents, asking if they had everything they needed. We had lots of food, for sure, but I wondered about my parents. My dad sat in the den a lot. My mom sat in a corner of the living room. Did we have everything we needed? What was going to happen next?

Mary Ann called me on Sunday and asked me when I was coming back to school. She added that it was the final week of *Julius Caesar* rehearsals. I had forgotten about it! Luckily, I hadn't missed it. Could I go to school on Monday? I didn't know. I wasn't sure whom I would ask. Surely somebody would tell me when to go back to school.

On Monday morning, neither of my parents said anything about school, and my sister and I slept late. We watched TV and read our books. We found ham sandwiches in the fridge at lunchtime and a pan of lasagna for dinner, but no one noticed we had run out of cereal and orange juice. That evening, we heard the kids outside playing kick the can. Deirdre and I looked at each other, into the dark rooms of our house, and then just walked out the door to go play. My parents didn't notice, so we figured it was fine.

Later that night, our neighbor, Mrs. Smith, called and said she'd pick my sister and me up at 10 a.m. to drive us to school for the dress rehearsal of *Julius Caesar*. She had one son in my class and one in Deirdre's. Mrs. Smith was the neighborhood mom who took all the children on our block to the Christmas pageant at St. Mary's and for cocoa and caroling afterwards. Although we played with her sons outside nearly every day, I don't recall seeing her in the springtime. I don't know how she knew to pick us up, or why Deirdre was coming too, but I didn't question it. I made sure my sister wasn't wearing pajamas, and that I had my script.

Mrs. Smith brought us up to the sixth-grade social studies room. Miss Godwin took my hands and spoke to me quietly, asking if I felt up to doing my part, or if I wanted to just watch. I didn't know if I was "up for it," but it seemed silly to be at school and not rehearse. I assured her that I was fine. In fact, I added, I'd had a lot of extra time to memorize the script. Her painful grimace made me realize I had possibly said something wrong. It wasn't even true, but I had thought it would make her feel better.

Being out in public was more complicated than I'd expected. There were reactions to navigate with adults that I was unprepared to tackle. My classmates, at least, were happy to see me back. Their easy smiles reassured me, and I did well with my lines and cues.

Deirdre was happy once she realized no one expected
her to do any schoolwork that day. The hour went by
quickly. Miss Godwin announced we would run through
the play one more time before lunch, but downstairs
on the gymnasium stage where the actual performance
would be! As she led us down, I saw Mr. McManus
step into the hall. I wanted to show him the toga they
made for me, but I wasn't supposed to step out of line. I
jumped up a little and waved to catch his attention. He
looked surprised to see me. He gave a quick wave and a
weak smile before darting back into his room. Once in
the gym, I saw several other teachers. My former third-
grade teacher ducked away as soon as she saw us. The
principal's secretary came right over and hugged me. The
gym teacher brought a ball over for Deirdre to play with
and asked if we needed anything else. Finally, our music
teacher murmured, "Please give my best to your mother."
How did she know my mother? I couldn't bear receiving
all this strained attention and unfamiliar pity. I quickly
did my part and wondered if I really had to come back to
school tomorrow.

On the drive home, Mrs. Smith suggested we stop at
the grocery store and pick up a couple of things for my
family. She said she had to stop anyway, and it would just
take a minute.

"What do you think you need?" she asked. I had no
idea, but she was looking so earnestly at me that I knew I
had to come up with something.

"Cereal and orange juice," Deirdre piped up.

"Sure, of course. Anything else? For dinner, maybe?"

"Um, maybe some hot dogs? And bread. My dad likes pumpernickel," I added, pleased at how considerate that last item sounded.

"Great!" she exclaimed with a little chuckle. "We will get all of that!" she assured me. Then I worried it sounded like I was asking for too much. She put her arm around my shoulder and said, "You must be a big help to your parents."

Yes, I guess I was. I scanned the shelves until I recognized the orange juice we usually bought. I sang the first name and last name of the hot dogs we ate, "O-S-C-A-R M-A-Y-E-R," and found them. There was only one kind of pumpernickel bread, so that was easy. The cereal aisle had several choices. My neighbor asked, "What kind of cereal do you and your sister like?"

Deirdre did not hesitate. "Lucky Charms!" she exclaimed. I stepped closer to the shelves and scanned them for the blue moons, pink stars, and green clovers. We usually had Cheerios, and I had only seen this coveted item on TV ads. As I scanned the shelves, a display of wholesome oat and raisin granola bags tripped me up. I closed my eyes over the tears. Whenever my brother came home, he brought us bags of granola, homemade and crunchy, from his commune's bakery. He extolled the benefits of natural foods and condemned the poisons in processed foods with artificial coloring and chemical additives. My stomach started to feel queasy, and I pulled at Mrs. Smith's hand.

"Can we go home now? Please?" I whispered, unsure if I could speak another word. The day suddenly felt

that it had been too long. It felt too normal, and now
too devoid of the family I used to have. What was I
doing here grocery shopping with a lady I hardly knew?
Buying junk food and forgetting about Mark? My
insides hurt, and I just wanted to get home.

A Time to Mourn

In 1969, Elisabeth Kübler-Ross published her seminal book, *On Death and Dying*, which proposed five stages of dying. The five stages of denial, anger, bargaining, depression, and acceptance were later applied to grieving as well, although perhaps not in a strictly linear manner. As I grappled with death growing up, I experienced these stages intimately, seeing them play out around me, feeling my way through them personally, and watching from a distance as my parents got mired in them.

Starting in junior high, I read everything I could about loss. It was helpful to know that the feelings I was feeling were to be expected. Someone had studied them and even explained that they could be useful. As I got older, though, I discovered one thing missing from the prescriptions of grief research. Knowing the stages is absolutely no help in getting through them. There aren't skills that can be employed to avoid the painful part. But it really helps if you have people supporting you and guiding you as you work through them.

In the late 1980s, when Kinsey died, I was living in another state with my new spouse Stephen. Kinsey and I had remained in touch as pen pals throughout my high school and college years. He was a smart man, father to a son who became a *New York Times* reporter and loving husband to a children's author. He encouraged me to seek out a Quaker meeting in my new home and felt great pleasure when I told him I was becoming a regular attendee. He and Eleanor came to my wedding and stood in as grandparents and elders at our Quaker-esque wedding in a field. He was an old man the whole time I knew him, but he finally got really old and died. I will never forget the day I heard he was dead, but not because of my grief.

After my mom's phone call with the news, I headed out to the park to meet several friends for a potluck picnic dinner we had planned. As I walked down the path, flanked by maples and aspens, I knew Kinsey would be glad I was outside in nature. After sharing beers, cold cuts, and potato salad with the group, I leaned over and asked Stephen if I could talk to him for a minute. We stepped off to the side, and I matter-of-factly shared the news of Kinsey's passing. Stephen bolted into the trees! I called his name and ran to catch up. He was leaning on a nearby trunk, heaving and weeping. The word "grief-stricken" came to me.

Kinsey was the first significant person to die in Stephen's life. The news of Kinsey's death clobbered him over the head and stabbed him quick in the heart, unexpected and brutal. He was feeling it all, powerfully. Unadulterated grief. Kubler-Ross and all the grief researchers had nothing useful to offer about this. Pain is pain. All they have to say is move through it and don't deny it.

Every death comes with pain. While one's own pain is intense, witnessing a loved one slammed by grief is equally rough. I can easily recall the reactions of friends and my helplessness when they received news of deaths. Stephen's grief in the woods. Or Kinsey's own, when his eighteen-year-old granddaughter died in a car accident by a drunk driver. A teaching colleague, whose husband shot himself shortly before their daughter's first birthday. My neighbor, whose husband stopped breathing suddenly one morning, even though we all thought his cancer treatments were working. My cousins, when their adult son was in hospice and died in their home. Mothers and fathers, sisters and brothers, spouses and friends, bereft when someone up and died. We grieve the deceased, but watching someone you love weep and break is its own agony.

Early in our marriage, we got a dog. Clara Bow was an important part of our family. My firstborn, Ben, grew up with her, hiked with her, snuck her dog bones, and threw her sticks in the river. One night, at the age of nine, Clara didn't eat her dinner, and then ignored her breakfast. So I took her to the vet while Ben was in school. Tests showed she had a tumor the size of a grapefruit and an irregular heartbeat. The vet kindly suggested I take her home, keep her hydrated, and over the weekend discuss how we would like to proceed. But in the few hours between leaving for the appointment and returning home, our dear Clara couldn't even get herself in and out of the car. I had to carry her ninety-pound body into the living room and figure out what to tell our son. Ben spent the afternoon at Clara's side, offering her ice to lick and dog bones she wouldn't take. I made Ben come into the kitchen to eat a sandwich for dinner. I told him we didn't know how much longer Clara had because she was very sick. She could die over the weekend, I said. He ran back to her side. Clara had drooled onto the rug. He lifted her head into his lap, and a strong smell of urine rose from underneath her. She convulsed and then did not move. I had never literally seen a living being die right before me. I, too, did not move. And then my sweet, blond-haired, kind-hearted little boy screamed and sobbed, his entire self shaking, involuntarily bawling. I held him, stroked him, stayed with him, but knew without a doubt that I was impotent in every way of alleviating his pain.

Grief, to me, is a noun. Mourning is a verb, an action word. Mourning is the variety of things that we do to get us through grief. Mourning may include having a wake, reading or writing sympathy cards, lighting a candle, sending or receiving flowers and casseroles, and all the things funeral directors guide you through.

In my adult life, many in my community use the same funeral home. I have been in the same room where my mother's calling hours were at least half a dozen other times since her death. It is surprisingly comforting. I know the way. The front door leads to a large beige and white room. The lectern at the door holds the guest book; small tables hold cherished photographs of the deceased. Floral arrangements line the back wall, with or without a casket. A hushed receiving line winds through it all, toward the grieving family, their water and tissues an arm's length away. The mourners exit through a side archway into another room with more photos and a slightly lighter air. Conversations start with memories of the deceased and move on to small talk and catching up among good friends and family. Regardless of circumstances, faith or non-faith, these rituals of death provide a way forward when all seems in chaos.

Moving forward is about all one can ask for. It may be slow going. It may be two steps forward and one step back. It may be forward steps that take you into a downward spiral until it looks like you are moving forward again. One day, one hour at a time.

4

The month of June brought us to the final weeks of school. My sister and I were now going every day. We walked to the school bus stop in the morning, careful not to miss it. There'd be no other way to get there. Dad couldn't drive us. I didn't know how to ask if he was sick or just not going to work. My mom usually made an appearance in the morning, still in her bathrobe. She wore the old cotton quilted robe that used to be worn only for dyeing her hair. The collar was bleached and spotted, and one pocket was ripped. I knew she had other robes, including a nylon and lace set we used to dress up in, but those stayed in the closet. She checked on us, put out a box of cereal, and then disappeared upstairs. We called out a goodbye as we headed out the front door for the bus stop.

One day after school, I found my dad asleep in front of the TV. A half-eaten sandwich and an empty tumbler were on the coffee table. He was sound asleep, but luckily not dead, which I had first thought. I couldn't find my mom anywhere. I looked throughout the house, even in the basement. I debated calling Mrs Smith, but I didn't know her phone number. I could have called Eleanor, but I didn't actually know what I'd say. My dad was there with us after all. Besides, after Mark moved to the commune, Deirdre and I often stayed at home alone for an hour or two until the library closed and my mom came home. Sure enough, at 5:30 p.m., my mom walked in the front door. She was in a sleeveless knit dress, stockings, and her sensible shoes. Her face looked beautiful again, and her hair was strawberry blond. She gave me a peck on the cheek and said dinner would be at 6:30 p.m. Then she walked into the kitchen. I stood frozen where she'd kissed me, feet rooted on the pale blue linoleum tile. Could it be? She had gone to work at the library that day? And dinner too? I skipped up the stairs to tell Deirdre.

The following week, my dad started back at work. He still didn't drive us to school, and he often stayed late at the office, but he went to work every day in a white shirt and tie. We had dinner every evening. We watched Carol Burnett on Friday night and went out for Jim Dandies on Saturday. I caught myself thinking about mundane things, like a Milton Bradley game I wanted and a cute boy at my bus stop. Deirdre and I went back to sleeping in separate rooms. I found I loved my privacy again, and I hung a tapestry from the top bunk down the wall side of the bed, making a cave to rest inside and covering the red wall.

At the end of the month, I would graduate from sixth grade. My friends and I were excited to head to junior high school in September. A new chapter for us! Looking ahead filled me with such unexpected joy. As we prepared to say goodbye to the school year, we also spoke of our summer plans. Mine brought the promise of a family camping trip, ballet camp, and hopefully weeks without crying.

My mother had been planning our summer vacation for months, long before their sudden trip to New Hampshire. I learned at dinner one night that we were still going! They had already purchased airplane tickets to Denver, Colorado. We had an RV reserved and waiting. We would spend two weeks in July winding through several Southwest states, visiting friends, and staying in campgrounds until we reached Las Vegas for the annual American Library Association (ALA) Conference.

Both of my parents were librarians. They had met as students at Northeastern University. My dad was there thanks to the GI Bill, and my mom was there thanks to her father, who pushed his firstborn to get a college education, even if she wasn't a boy. Two decades later, my mother was the head children's librarian in our small suburban town, running story hours, book clubs, and after-school programs. My dad used his training to get a job as the first archivist at the new corporate headquarters of IBM. At work, he preserved the history and legacy of the Watson family, who had run IBM for half a century. At home, he introduced us to a world of technology and corporate loyalty. We used paper punch cards for scrap paper and played on a Braille typewriter and the new-fangled Selectric ball cartridge typewriter. We followed the Apollo missions as if we had a direct link to the command center, since IBM computers were making them possible. We went to annual company picnics and executive holiday events, with visits from Santa. We had taken other vacations organized around the ALA annual meeting, once in New York and then Atlantic City, but this summer was to be a big splurge. We would travel in RV luxury and fly on an airplane! My father insisted we deserved it. I heard him repeat this again and again as we traveled.

We did everything my mother had planned. Everything was as planned, except without Mark. No one ever mentioned that he was supposed to be traveling with us. Most of the time it was okay. We picked up a van-sized RV in Boulder and drove off to see canyons and mesas in Arizona, met our Hopi and Navajo pen pals, and stood on the Four Corners with each appendage in a different state. When we stopped at an old friend's house, I noticed sudden looks between my parents and a turn in the conversation. Time to take my sister and disappear for a little while. No one had to tell me to go play, because I certainly preferred it to hearing the private conversation of adults bemoaning our family's tale of woe. The rest of the visit was gleeful, sometimes excessively so, as Jim Beam lubricated my parents' vacationing. We drove on and floated in the Salton Sea, baked in Needles, California, and finally arrived in Las Vegas.

Tension grew in the car as we drove onto the garish neon strip. I was sad we were at the end of our adventure, but I wasn't really sure why everything suddenly was taking a turn for the worse. We checked in and put on smiles in the bustling hotel. My parents dressed up very fancy for a big banquet and told Deirdre and me that we would have to stay in the hotel room. We were ecstatic! We ordered pizza, drank soda, and watched TV for hours while they attended their boring dinner. It was a high point of the trip!

Long after we were supposed to be asleep, we heard their voices out in the hallway. We quickly shut off the TV and dove under the sheets together.

"… none of their business!" My mom's voice was shrill and growly.

"… good friend … come on …" My dad's voice was pleading and slurred.

As their key unlocked the knob, we froze and feigned sleep. Deirdre might have even snored.

"I don't want to talk about it all with everyone. We can't." Without a break in her diatribe, my mother lifted me out of one double bed and placed me in the empty one. "You know that!"

"Come on … it's not a big deal," he pleaded.

She loudly said good night to my father and got into the bed beside me. She rolled over toward the wall, and there was not another sound all night. I was awake for most of it, so I know.

Cullinane family circa 1963

That's me!

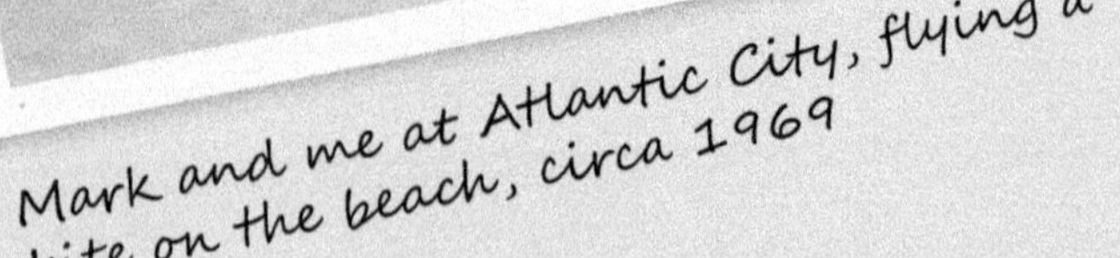

Mark and me at Atlantic City, flying a
kite on the beach, circa 1969

My dad, Eddie Cullinane, date unknown

Deirdre and me with Sammy
at our house, circa 1970–72

Mark's senior
year photo,
1971

Mark & Leslie
New Hampshire
1972

grandparents'
headstone

my sixth-grade class photo, 1972–73

me

Mom, Eleanor, Deirdre, Kinsey & me, late 1970s

Mom and me, circa 1981

5

There was another plan made a lifetime before. The previous winter I had lobbied heavily to go to the Istvan Rabovsky Ballet Camp with my friend Paula. I loved to dance, and had taken ballet at our local community hall for a couple of years. I pleaded that I must have serious training. The camp, located in the Catskills, advertised a rewarding and constructive summer for young girls. The brochure Paula showed me was filled with bucolic scenery and girls in leotards everywhere. My parents had consented and paid the deposit back in February. Arriving home from Las Vegas, however, I was less enthusiastic. I felt weary, physically and emotionally. We all were, but we moved forward with the plan. Doing laundry, sewing name tags onto my leotards, packing the items from the camper list, and buying stamps for sending postcards home. It seemed easier to just do it than to navigate complicated conversations.

I loved Rabovsky's, and I hated it. The tough Russian training felt serious and consuming. I enjoyed the intense focus, morning to night. We did, in fact, dance everywhere—in the mirrored studio, on the pathways, draped across the porches of the painted gingerbread cabins. The visuals were cute. The girls? Beautiful,

talented, carefree, and not like me at all. My memories
of camp are of being very lonely. I wrote home daily,
asking for more stamps and money for the commissary,
and asking about my dog, my sister, and everyone I
could think of. I applied myself all day at the classes and
rehearsals, and I wept silently into my pillow at night.

The day I arrived, I was caught unprepared when
a bunkmate asked if I had siblings. I blurted out that I
had one sister, period. Omission was an easier way to
lie. Later, another girl asked, and I felt obligated to be
consistent. She rambled that she only had brothers and
hated them and wished she had a sister. Another girl
chimed in and said she had one of each, and liked her
sister better too! Their chatter swirled around the bunk.
I noticed my friend from home on her bed overhearing
us. Paula caught my eye and flashed a pitying look,
friendly and understanding. She said nothing. It made
me feel wretched! The opportunity to correct my lie
passed, and I lived the next couple of weeks in denial. I
had betrayed my brother's existence, and it hadn't even
helped me.

I was miserable. I wanted a hug from my mother. I
wanted to walk downtown, holding my father's hand.
I wanted to snuggle with my sister and to know that
she was doing okay. I felt vulnerable in this new place
where no one knew me. I tried to find comfort in the
wildflowers, by eating granola each morning, chanting in
my head a Sanskrit verse Mark used to sing, and writing
those daily postcards home. *HOW ARE YOU??* The
ballet classes were absorbing, but the thought that kept

repeating in my head was, *You'd really like it here if you weren't so sad.*

A Time to Embrace

The same year *On Death and Dying* was published, a dozen women met in a workshop titled "Women and Their Bodies," which catapulted into the formation of the Boston Women's Health Collective and finally the publication of *Our Bodies, Ourselves.* These two books, along with Marlo Thomas' children's book *Free to Be … You and Me,* came into my home after my brother died. Clearly, there was synergy in the air. Feelings mattered. Everyone counted. Saying how you felt was important. Strong feelings should be acknowledged. Really sad, strong feelings were normal. It's alright to cry.

And after crying, there needs to be a hug. It is the embrace that has brought me the most support. Hugging is the one thing, the only thing, that I can say helps. Whether it is because of the sheer physical sense of touch, the releasing of endorphins noted to be found in a twenty-second hug, or the holding of someone else's burdens, however briefly, hugging a person through grief works. I have been both the receiver and the giver. I have been the casual friend and the best friend, the mourning daughter and the fellow survivor. Offering an embrace helps when words fall short, when promises of better days sound false, and when the loss is so profound that taking a friend in arms is the clearest way to express, *I am here with you.*

Every death is an experience of loss. There is no ranking system, but some say anticipating a death, like with Alzheimer's disease or cancer, may help ease the pain. With long illnesses, grief starts even before death and then again after, but grief still drives its course. With a tragic, sudden death, grief comes at full speed and throws you off the cliff.

I have spent years trying to untangle my brother's story, posing questions, reading, journaling, and talking with therapists. I want to offer something profound to surviving family members and friends. I bond with those who have experienced tragic loss, whether through suicide, accidents, abrupt fatal conditions, or unexpected downturns when recovery seemed likely. I am a bit of a death junkie, I guess. Death is one time when I show up. It is a life event I know something about, so I want to help. When friends have a loss, I go to the funeral home, read the obituary, attend the funeral, visit the gravesite, and send a sympathy card. The rituals are a time of shared grief, not just for the recently deceased but for all the losses a community or family has withstood together. I have mined them, as they are an incredibly rich resource of wisdom and coping.

In particular, there is a powerful alliance among people who have lost a loved one to suicide. News of that kind of death is terribly sudden, crushing, and fraught with questions and guilt for the survivors. I am familiar with the dialogue that takes place, internally and publicly. *What do you mean?* One day we were together, and the next they were dead. A husband, a father, a brother, a roommate, another brother, a child, a neighbor. *How did they do it?* A gun, a rope, a fire, a boat, pills. *Did they mean it?* I don't know. They killed themselves. *How could I not know? Why didn't they tell me? Did they tell me?* Questions without answers, without end. When I hear of someone in my community who has been affected by suicide, I ache for all the grief ahead. I feel all the grief behind me. My heart splits open. Literally, as the teenagers say. My chest feels torn apart and I thank God for ribs to hold it all together.

With years of outreach and receiving, learning and watching, I have found that 99 percent of the time, hugging is the only reasonable thing to do. A hug is the rib cage. Embracing someone is the closest I can get to being their rib cage, to hold them together, at least for a moment. Grief support is less about removing pain and more about holding life together.

Embracing is an instinctual expression of love. When faced with even potential loss, we crave the reassurance of an embrace. My list of deaths would not be complete without the Almost Deaths. A whole page just for those events when, thank God, there wasn't a death. A close call, a stroke of luck, found soon enough, left soon enough, happened to someone else ...

In high school, my boyfriend was in a high-speed car accident when his parents thought he was home in bed.

The car was totaled; he broke his leg and several ribs, and the friendships in that car were ruined. His parents have never forgotten the panic they felt when they received a phone call telling them their son in the emergency room was seriously injured. In the weeks that followed, as his parents nursed him back to health in their living room, his mother mostly felt grateful that he lay there, physically present even in his brokenness. She felt more grateful than angry, disappointed, or displeased with his reckless and irresponsible behavior. She touched him every time she walked by: a hand on his hand, a squeeze of his shoulder, a pat on his back, a stroke of his bangs. When he became more mobile, she hugged him every time he went out. I was not a parent then, but I totally get it now.

I have been a parent in the emergency room. I have received phone calls. Whether or not I believe in a higher power, I have thanked God that my child or loved one still lives, breathes, and populates this earth. I have hugged my child, stretching my arms around cuts and IV tubes. I once snuggled onto a skinny ambulance stretcher to hold and breathe sustenance into my delirious elderly mother when she misdosed her medication and spent hours in and out of consciousness. And each time violence has erupted in our country, randomly ending some lives and traumatizing others inside a movie theater, a classroom, or a concert, I have wrapped my arms around my loved ones, just hugging, silently reassuring myself that we are safe and whole.

A dear friend whose middle-aged son died suddenly of a heart attack carries on each day because of the hugs she has received from friends and family. Physical hugs received at home, virtual hugs posted online, long-distance hugs from friends gathering in her son's name. His absence from this world cannot be altered, but those hugs are prayers, commitments to carry on her son's bigheartedness and to grow the bonds of his love. Holding tightly to one another and offering condolences are not trite social niceties. Hugs express more than words can articulate.

At almost twelve, I didn't have any idea what would help me feel better, but every time my mom or dad or anyone gave me a hug, I felt maybe it was going to be okay.

6

Autumn is my favorite month. It always has been. After the stress of that summer, I looked forward to doing all the fall things—jumping in piles of leaves with Deirdre, going hiking with my dad on the Appalachian Trail, collecting maple leaves and ironing them between wax paper sheets so my mom could hang them on the library children's room windows, and celebrating my birthday in October.

For my twelfth year, my dad gave me a leather diary with a gold lock. For one of my first entries, I wrote, "I vow to write only happy thoughts and good memories in this diary! My life is going to be good, good, good!!" I loved exclamation marks! I consciously launched myself into the school year. The previous spring had been so low that I figured everything would head upward from then on. I welcomed the new school, new grade, and new routines. The bus ride to my regional junior high was longer, but I told myself it just gave me time to read or finish homework. The bus came earlier, and my bus stop was farther away. So I found an alarm clock in the attic and set it every morning. I was learning to be responsible and to plan ahead. I found positive ways to look at life's little problems.

In seventh grade, I made new friends, kept the old ones, learned my way around the new building, and liked most of my teachers. We had many teachers in middle school. Luckily, I got to have my most favorite teacher twice, for science and study hall. I loved being in her room! She had gotten married that summer and told us her new name was Mrs. Kruchkow. She talked about her husband and the books she read, as well as telling us the parts of a flower and good local hikes. She let us write poems, do macrame, organize lab equipment, or sometimes do homework. With earnest concentration, she read my poems and never offered a word of correction. She would offer comments like, "You have such a tender heart" or "You describe the clouds so well." A few girls and I became her groupies. Being at school was wonderful! As much as possible, I tried to carry that home with me. I wrote each evening in my diary about all the happy events of the day.

Like all hip 1970s gals, I was passionate about arts and crafts. Creative expression! I was often doing some kind of handicraft—sewing a pillow, embroidering my jeans, watercoloring a bookmark, or stenciling a bookcase. One weekend, my parents went away to Boston together, the city they were both originally from. My mother even had a job interview there. My sister and I stayed with neighbors Jim and Jane and their six-month-old. We helped with adorable baby Julian, who was learning to crawl, while Jane cooked us dinner. On Sunday morning, she helped us with a decoupage project, a surprise wedding anniversary present for our parents. We sanded down an old wooden box and cut out flowers from a greeting card. She showed us how to glue the paper, sand it lightly, and cover with a varnish to make a beautiful box lid. A new craft for me!

Later, at home, I replicated the process, decoupaging the sympathy card from Mary Ann into a shadow box I had been putting together. I had created four interior sections to hold some of Mark's things—a pinch candle, an ID bracelet, some thistle from our yard, and a Chinese dog figurine he'd left in his drawer. The card was just the right touch for the center. "Sometimes the whole world seems depopulated …" I nailed a picture frame on top of the large outside box, careful to not crack the glass. It looked just how I had hoped it would!

My shadow box kept my memories displayed, but contained, neat, tender, and beautiful. I propped it up on my dresser and touched it each morning on my way out of the room. It was my mezuzah—I live here with you, and you live inside of me. It allowed me to honor Mark's life each day, to not forget him, but it also kept the grief, confusion, and chaos trapped inside and silent. I touched it, nodded, and went on with my day.

That year was all about music too. I had a round, bright-green transistor radio. At sleepovers, I sang with my friends. I rummaged in my dad's record closet. My dad was a huge folk fan, introducing me to Joan Baez, Judy Collins, and the rugged Bob Dylan. He shared snippets about himself as a young man in 1950s Boston and Philadelphia, hanging out in bookstores and cafes, soaking in the vibe, snapping to the Beat poets, and buying up the newest chapbooks. There was a stereo in our den and shelves of LPs, as well as a Victrola with thick 78 records of Muddy Waters, Count Basie, and the Weavers. My dad frequently left for hours on the weekend to scour garage sales for great record and book deals, among other things. His love for music lasted long after his love for most other things faded. I remember sitting beside him, sharing the shock of the news of Jim Croce's sudden death. With the rest of the country, we listened over and over to "Time in a Bottle," whose lyrics were now all the more prophetic.

> *If I could save time in a bottle*
> *The first thing that I'd like to do*
> *Is to save every day*
> *Till eternity passes away*
> *Just to spend them with you*
> —Jim Croce

I knew music had been important to my brother. In fact, Mark had snuck out to Woodstock at the age of fifteen, catching a ride with some older friends. I don't remember being told any more, but that must have been quite an adventure! His groovy friends listened to *Shootout at the Fantasy Factory* by Traffic, *Quadrophenia* by The Who, and *The Dark Side of the Moon* by Pink Floyd. I pretended to like them, but at twelve, I was more interested in The Partridge Family, The Osmonds, and The Banana Splits. I did like the pop star Elton John, whose *Don't Shoot Me I'm Only the Piano Player* had come out at the beginning of 1973. Radio stations pushed hit after hit off that album, like "Crocodile Rock" and "Elderberry Wine." Throughout my seventh-grade year, radio stations increasingly played "Daniel." My sister and I sang along, allowing the lyrics to say things for us that we felt we shouldn't speak. We belted out the words, and no one had to know what meaning they held for us.

> *Daniel, my brother, you were older than me,*
> *Do you still feel the pain*
> *of the scars that won't heal?*
> *Your eyes have died,*
> *but you see more than I,*
> *Daniel, you're the star*
> —Elton John

After school, I volunteered at my elementary school, a clever plan my mother finagled to fill the void of after-school care providers. Hardly any of my friends' mothers worked outside the home at that time. I helped my former music teacher, Miss Milligan, a couple of afternoons a week, straightening supplies and keeping her company. She was as cool and even younger than my science teacher! In sixth grade, she often kept the textbooks closed, handed out percussion instruments, and asked us to close our eyes and play along with a rock LP. She even had us decipher the lyrics of Cat Stevens' "Moonshadow" for a test grade. She inspired me to make my first record purchase, saving my allowance for weeks till I had enough to buy *Tommy, The Rock Opera* by The Who. By the end of the year, thanks to the mail-order Columbia Record Club and some babysitting, I owned all of Cat Stevens' albums, as well as a potpourri of Stevie Wonder, Barry Manilow, the Beatles, John Denver, Wings, Joni Mitchell, and Chicago. I had loud favorites for public listening, and quiet favorites for in-the-dark private listening.

Listening to music gave me the space to cry. I connected cathartically to ballads and sad, haunting lyrics, playing songs like Cat Stevens' "How Can I Tell You" and "Sad Lisa" over and over on my stereo. And crafting beautiful things, writing poetry, or being outside in nature filled me with happiness. My family and I made it through the end of 1973 pretty well.

7

Then we hit a bump. We had clung to typical routines—until we couldn't. Underneath our attempts at healing, there was a growing hollow shadow left in the place of Mark's living and breathing, laughing and shining presence. He wouldn't saunter into the house, like on his last visit, wool poncho smelling of bread-baking and incense (and marijuana, which I didn't recognize at the time). He wouldn't be tickling Deirdre and me till we couldn't breathe, or take us to his friend Alan's house instead of babysitting us at home. He didn't call or write or suddenly appear. Although he hadn't lived at home since graduating high school, he always came home. Now he didn't come for my birthday, or Thanksgiving, or Christmas. A darkness kept returning until it couldn't be avoided. It was like a pothole in the road that you try to anticipate on your way home, and then end up blowing your tire on it the next day.

My parents sat us down for a talk. Another one. Even before hearing a single word, I wanted the speech to be over. I did not feel well. My parents were strained and this time fakely chipper. Mom patted my knee and said, "It's good news, sweetie." Dad looked encouraging and reminded us about the job notice he'd seen in the paper.

"Well, your mother was offered that job in Boston, and took it! We are very happy for her," he said, beaming at her.

She quickly filled in, "But don't you worry. We aren't going to uproot you during the school year." The conversation jumped around, and finally I could go up to my room. What had just happened? I felt like Winnie the Pooh when he sits on his doorstep and says to himself, "Think, think, think."

My mom was starting a new job in another city in a few weeks. Deirdre and I would live with my dad in our house for six months without my mother. We would move to Boston the following summer and start at a new school next fall. This would be good for everybody, a small, ordinary adjustment, all for the better, and we would be happier.

My chest constricted, feeling as tight as when I had asthma attacks as a small child. I closed my eyes and bit my lip. My brain flooded like a car engine, unable to power on. I repeated their explanation to myself and struggled to decipher what it would be like. I didn't know how to put a spin on this that would make it seem right. I couldn't tell if it was a beginning or an end; it felt like both. I really didn't feel well.

My mother did what she always did. She made lists and organized us. I did what made sense in that moment; I read the lists, followed instructions, and did what was expected of me. She made sure I knew where the extra blankets were, who to call in an emergency, and which weekends she would be back for visits.

She taught me how to cook five dinners. Dad
would take care of the weekend meals. I listened
carefully, absorbed her advice, and practiced each
meal once before she moved out. Using ground beef,
ketchup, bread crumbs, and an egg (which she told
me to keep secret), I prepared meatloaf. I baked pork
chops, slathered in ketchup ("easier than making a
marinade") and nestled into chopped-up potatoes.
I boiled spaghetti, throwing a strand at the cabinet
to see if it was done ("throw another for fun"). I
scrambled five eggs ("because your dad likes them")
and fried some frozen sausage links. We were running
out of preparation time, so the fifth meal became ham
sandwiches. A sandwich for dinner? I managed to
tell her I didn't want to practice making a sandwich.
It seemed too sad to have sandwiches for our final
meal. It had, in fact, been fun spending time with
my mom while she taught me to cook … but … She.
Was. Leaving.

I didn't want to be her friend anymore. I didn't want
to be good at cooking and being responsible. I wanted
my mom to stay. Why did she have to move away? I
wanted her to hug me every morning.

But she left. And the school bus came early, as always,
every Monday through Friday. It drove right past my
house on the way to the bus stop. That midwinter,
on more than one occasion, I heard the bus from the
kitchen and flew out the front door, racing along just

behind it for three blocks to the bus stop. My new alarm clock didn't always wake me up. My dad didn't tell us to go to bed at night, and I often read until very late. Dad was usually asleep himself right after dinner, in front of the TV with a whisky tumbler at his side. Sometimes, we would sneakily change the station to watch a show we liked, instead of the news.

Sometimes Dad wouldn't be home for dinner. My mom told me to make it ready for six o'clock each night. I did. If he wasn't there, I'd wait a few minutes and then tell my sister we might as well eat it while it's hot, hearing my mother's voice guiding me. We left a full plate on the table for him. Sometimes it was there the next morning, and I'd scrape it into the garbage. I'd find him in the den usually, in an undershirt and underwear, sprawled on the couch, TV on. It was a relief to see him there; he always came home. I heard of other dads who sometimes didn't.

Those several months were a long stretch. Both parents were falling apart. They were each drinking copiously, staying angry and acutely sad. Deirdre and I had little supervision and could do anything, but we mostly did nothing. Once, she ran away. Once, I locked myself in the attic. Twice, we poured water into my dad's bottle of bourbon. Sometimes, I snuck into his treasured record closet and borrowed his Dylan and Mama Cass albums; he never noticed.

There were good days, mostly on the weekend visits—when my dad pretended he was a race car driver in our station wagon on the Mass Pike with all the windows down, or when my mom took us on a shopping spree in Filene's Basement for spring clothes and we watched old ladies in their brassieres trying on blouses, or best of all, when we all went out to Friendly's for Jim Dandies again. Once, we saw my mom and dad holding hands on a walk downtown.

One Saturday in April, my mom changed her plans and didn't visit. I worried that my dad would be upset. Instead, he took me with him to scout out thrift sales. He loved a good bargain! We used to do this a lot in the *before* times. It is how he built his record collection, furnished our basement, and once surprised my mom with a fur coat.

"Look at this beauty!" he exclaimed. It was a leather-bound, gilded volume of poetry. He opened it up to discover ripped and water-stained pages. "What a shame …" He put it back on the table. We kept looking through the tables. He wandered deep into the church basement. Awhile later, I heard him call my name.

"Maeve, come over here. Look at this!" He stood before a beautiful, antique leather trunk with massive hinges. It reminded me of pictures I'd seen of travelers in the late 1800s getting on board a train or ship with their earthly belongings packed in these large cases.

"Would you like this?" he asked. He lifted the lid for me, showing the linen-covered interior and the lift-out trays dividing the voluminous insides. "You could put your trousseau in it," he said and winked at me. I felt so grown-up in that moment. This was not a toy or tchotchke.

"I love it!" I replied and wrapped my arms around him in a big bear hug. It took two other men to help load it into our Chevy station wagon. Every time I have moved it since, I've marveled at its sheer weight and my dad's determination and glee to get it for me.

8

The one-year anniversary of Mark's death was bound to come. The month of May felt ominous. One weekend, my sister and I went to Boston without my dad, taking the train together. My mom met us at South Station, and we splurged on a taxi to her apartment in Back Bay. Deirdre and I talked a mile a minute about all the things we'd done with friends, TV shows we watched, and people we met on the train. Mom listened to every word, interested and happy. She was much more relaxed in Boston. But as soon as dinner was over, it was time for another sit-down talk. I assumed it would be about the anniversary, but no. She did not talk about Mark; she never did. She casually told us that after the school year was over, we would move in with her, but Dad wouldn't come to Boston. She would get an apartment for the three of us and settle my sister and me into a good school in Brookline. Dad needed to stay to sell the house, take some time, figure out what to do in Boston, and such. My mom's voice rambled on, very matter of fact and reasonable, with explanation after explanation. I felt like she wasn't telling us something.

The question in my head was, "Are you getting divorced?" but instead, I said, "I'm really tired. Can I go to bed?"

The following week back at home, while spring flowers brightened my yard, I lay in bed. I told my dad I was sick. I missed a week of school. I watched PBS all day, catching the instructional programs for science and social studies so I wouldn't fall behind. My neighbor Randy brought me home the math and English worksheets. Maybe I really was sick. I was so tired that I often fell asleep with schoolwork on my lap. My dad took me to the doctor's office twice, the second time to get blood drawn. I was scared, partly because of the needles and partly because of worrying about why they needed to check my blood. My dad acted as if nothing that was happening was a big deal. I whispered to Mark's spirit one night, willing my big brother to be my ally again and help me through this mess.

When the lab results came back, my dad told me, "Well, the good thing about mono is that it isn't contagious. As soon as you have your energy back, you can go to school. And even better, no gym for a month!"

"What is mono?" I asked.

"Nothing to worry about. You just need more rest. I will get dinner, and you can sleep all day. Mom will be home tomorrow to take care of you."

Mom? Tomorrow will be Tuesday. Now I was really worried. Why would Mom come in the middle of the week? I tossed in bed worrying, drifted to sleep, nibbled at a sandwich, worried, and slept well into the next morning.

Late that afternoon, my mom was there on the edge of my bed, fully explaining mononucleosis to me.

She brought me an extra pillow and a glass of water.
She tucked the sheet under my shoulders and asked,
"Feel better?" With no need for an answer, she started
reading aloud a chapter from one of the Newbery Award
nominees she was evaluating. I started to doze. She kissed
me on the forehead and gently closed my door. I sank into
the pillow and let the warmth consume me. I guess I did
just need more sleep. Her light footsteps headed down the
stairs. Not more than ten minutes later, I jolted awake.

"God damn it, Ed!" My mother never swore.

"… leave me here. What do you expect?" My dad
was yelling.

"… can't depend … anything!!"

"… my best …" Our back door slammed.

I pulled my blanket over my head and squished up
against the red wall. I hummed to myself, "Oh, I'm
being followed by a moon shadow, moon shadow, moon
shadow," until I fell back to sleep.

With only a few more weeks left of school, I finally
returned. A doctor's note excused me from gym, and my
teachers gave me an entire week to make up the missed
work. They were all very understanding. Very. When I
heard the bus turn onto my road the next morning, I ran
to the front door and froze. The bus had stopped right at
my door. The driver cranked open the accordion doors
and waved me in.

"Come on. Come on!" she called jovially. "Now
remember, you shouldn't run."

"Okay," I responded in surprise.

In a hushed voice, she added, "I can't drop you here in the afternoon, but I will stop every morning for ya, sweetie."

"Oh. Okay … um, thank you," I said, realizing I didn't know her name.

"Happy to help … you have a lot on your shoulders," and she looked back to the steering wheel and closed the door.

I sat several rows behind her without meeting the eyes of the other kids. Gazing out the window, I looked up into the woods where Kinsey and I had walked. I looked at each house on my street as we drove by them. I thought about my neighbors, the cashier at the grocery store, the ladies who worked with my mom at the library, all of my teachers, this bus driver. Did they all know? Not just about my mono.

Did they know I had a brother who died? What had they heard? What did they think? Did they know my mother lived in Boston now? They did, didn't they? Did they know about my dad? I was overcome by the realization that my private pain and my family's instability were completely public! The excessive kindness was them taking pity on me! I didn't know whether I felt embarrassed or pathetic or furious. Who knew what? Who thought what? No one said anything. I had been miserable and alone, clasping my feelings tightly to me, keeping them small and in my shadow box, while my neighbors, everyone around me, watched and thought, *how sad, how awful, poor girl.*

I hated that idea. I knew then I wanted to be fine every single day, and do everything right and good, and show everyone that my life was not something to pity. My brother was the best human being in the world. My family was not some sad assemblage of broken people. I needed the world to see me as whole and filled with light. I walked off the bus with all the other kids and chirpily told the bus driver, "Have a nice day!"

Note: *The next section contains an explicit discussion of suicide. It is not overtly graphic, but should be read gently.*

A Time to Speak

The truth is, no one wants to talk about death or loss. We don't know how to have conversations about pain. It is difficult to be open to pain, either as part of mourning or as part of living. And when someone is in pain, deep pain that alters their daily perspective, most conversations feel superficial, or miss the mark, or hold triggers and daggers that make things worse.

After my brother died, I'd hear my mother say she had two daughters or, "We're a family of four." It irked me. It wasn't untrue, but it wasn't true. I tried in my adolescent mind to untangle the social mess of it all. We were a family of five, but then it became four. They had one son, then no sons. I had two siblings, then only a sister. I was the middle child, and now the oldest. The dynamics and order of my family had changed, and innocuous questions became less easy to answer. The very story of my parents' lives was rewritten. Without that first son, it looked like my parents had waited a long time into their marriage to have children, when really, they had had a baby boy as soon as they married and clung to their beautiful only child for eight years before hoping maybe another baby would be a good idea. That story stopped being told, and my mother simply said, "I have two daughters; Maeve is

my oldest." This answer kept chitchat superficial and far
from the landmine of death. We had become a different
family, one that none of us recognized, people who lived
with a secret, in a world depopulated because their Mark
was gone.

Worst of all, once I heard my father say his son was
in a car accident. By saying that, other adults could nod
and offer condolences. No fault or guilt or questions
with a car accident. He could move on. It made me
angry. The sympathy he received was wrong. He lied. It
seemed sacrilegious to lie in that way about my brother's
death. No version of my brother's death could ever be
considered a car accident. There was a car, but it was
actually a truck, and it was not moving. It was set on fire.
The accident part was debatable and not all that clear,
but even if I granted my dad the leeway to say "accident,"
my brother did not die in a car accident. These details
mattered tremendously to me for a long time.

Eventually, the details mattered not at all. The details
made nothing clearer, in fact. Pain and truth have a
tough time coexisting. I find pain usually takes the upper
hand, even with the best of intentions. Bereavement
support groups, therapy, and peers with common
experiences of loss have helped me speak the truth and
see its complexity.

My brother died by his own hand over five decades
ago, and there are multiple versions to explain what
happened. The facts of what happened are just one
version. There is also what my parents believed
happened, what my parents wanted to believe happened,

what my parents told us had happened, what my brother's community saw, and even what clues my brother's belongings suggested. As a young adult, I believed if I looked at all of these versions head-on, somewhere there would be The Truth. Somewhere there would be Mark, and I would understand. That understanding, in fact, continued to be elusive.

The summer before I left for college, my mother asked Deirdre and me to sit down on her bed. It was time for another talk. "I want to talk about Mark," stated my mom. My sister and I were all ears. This was a subject she never brought up. It had been six years since she told us my brother died accidentally in a fire. Now divorced and in her fifties, my mother was reinventing her life and attempting to free herself of the demon of secrecy. Maybe her therapist suggested it; maybe she was desperate to speak the words aloud. By not telling her young daughters about her son's suicide, she had walled herself off from talking about it with anyone. She sat us down to tell us "the truth." With little preamble, she launched into her statement.

"Mark set himself on fire behind the commune where he lived by pouring gasoline on himself and a truck. It was an act of self-immolation. He died quickly."

Outside, the traffic rumbled by, and I could hardly breathe. My sister asked something, which I barely heard. My mother responded, "I saw his body at the morgue, and he looked like marble."

I grabbed my sister's hand. The version of Mark working on a truck and accidentally starting a fire was not true. Deirdre looked at me and raised her eyebrows, as if to say, "I knew it." We had never mentioned to one another any doubts or questions about how our brother died, but we had each sensed that there was more than what we had been told. Now that my mother had shared her facts, we could speak aloud our thoughts and feelings. This changed everything.

Speaking began to heal us. My mother explained that on the drive back from New Hampshire, after identifying the body, my parents decided they couldn't bear to have their two little girls' lives shattered by a suicide. They decided that telling us it was an accident would preserve our love for Mark. They decided on this course of action while they were deeply in their own shock and pain, struggling also with the social stigma and sin of suicide. I imagine it felt like one small piece they could control.

My sister and I told my mother that we knew. My mother was relieved. I said we knew and we didn't know. I felt compelled to revisit pieces of the story with this new lens. We talked into the evening about Mark's friends at the commune that my parents had met. We agreed to invite his special friend, Leslie, to come visit. We talked about why we hadn't had a Catholic Mass and the decision to bury my brother's ashes in my grandfather's casket a year later. We didn't talk about everything, but we talked about a lot. It was a tremendous relief to lay down the secrecy. Still, it was not the complete truth.

Suicide, even without the stigma, is full of mystery. There's always the "why." It is the pivotal question for those dealing with the ripples of self-inflicted death.

Mental illness, chemical imbalance, hopelessness, isolation, self-loathing, and unbearable pain may be part of the answer. People who have attempted suicide and lived have much to contribute, even though the details may be different and perhaps not universal. Many who have survived say they are deeply, deeply appreciative that they are now alive, that something or someone intervened to keep them alive. One man who jumped off the Golden Gate Bridge spoke with other survivors of the same attempt, and almost all of them said there was enough time between leaving the railing and hitting the water for them to regret taking this step.

Ouch.

Why did Mark kill himself? My brother may have had schizophrenia or a psychotic break. In hindsight, my mother wondered about some instances of him as a younger teen when he seemed "troubled." He was never treated for any mental health issues, although my genetic line is replete with diagnoses from depression to bipolar to alcoholism throughout generations. It is certainly possible that Mark was afflicted. He also smoked pot and dropped acid, and both may increase the risk of psychosis. That could be a reason.

Another reason? My brother was immersed in the counterculture of the 1970s, beyond the drugs; he lived off the land in a commune, opposed the Vietnam War, and questioned the status quo. He wrote abstractly about higher purposes and transcendent experiences, and drew sketches in the margins of his journal of flames and drowning men. He told his sisters not to do heroin or eat chemicals or hold on to other people's anger. At ten years old, he saw a Buddhist monk symbolically immolate himself in the middle of Saigon to oppose the war. He looked up to draft dodgers just a little older than him and praised the burning of draft cards. He learned Bhajan Sanskrit chants and shunned materialism. He believed in reincarnation and spoke of "crossing this great ocean of birth and death." So did many others of his generation, who are senior citizens now. My mother clung to this spiritual explanation into her own old age, feeling this was the most comprehensible reason to believe why he would end his life. It was magnanimous, I suppose.

Had my brother planned his suicide? Did he have a moment of regret? Did his pain at the end cancel his days of happiness? Is his cause of death more significant somehow than his living? Did he think about how we would miss him?

This is what happens with suicide. Questions. Questions without answers.

The questions ripple through the lives of loved ones who must continue without answers. I have been in suicide support groups where we can talk and not shock one another with our stories. In college, I knew two women whose fathers had killed themselves, and that common experience single-handedly bridged the many differences between them. I have corresponded with other sisters of suicide, and we write about the siblings who are not getting older with us. I keep in touch with a former colleague whose husband shot himself in their own home, leaving behind his one-year-old daughter. I

have shared poetry with a man who found a housemate
hanging in a closet. My neighbor and I knew a young girl
who went to school with our children, and then one day
took her life. I have a dear friend whose only brother shot
himself at his desk a year after he got married. The new
thinking is that people no longer kill themselves. It is their
brain that pushes them out of life, like a diseased organ
that stops working properly. Something to think about …

Perhaps the simplest answer about my brother's death
I have had all along, like Dorothy who could always go
home with a click of her slippers. My big brother Mark's
life ended at the age of twenty. For whatever reason. I
care more about what he meant to me than why he went
away. I am almost seventy, and I wish I could talk with
him. There is an entire person who could have been in my
life for decades, and he was not. That is what I grieve.

> *I long to tell you*
> *That I'm always thinking of you*
> *I'm always thinking of you*
> *But my words just blow away*
> *Just blow away*
> —Cat Stevens

Years ago, I went to a revival of the cult film *Harold
and Maude*. It came out in 1971, and I had avoided it,
knowing it was full of antics around suicide and humor
about death and dying. Feeling ready to handle it, I sat in
the theater and braced myself. The very first notes of the

soundtrack hit me hard. It was Cat Stevens, my go-to music for cathartic sadness. I forced myself to breathe. I hated the movie, and loved it. It felt both caustic and healing to me in a way that I couldn't put words to. I walked out of the theater humming to Cat Stevens, exhausted and raw, and light on my feet. I find myself consciously embracing sadness and speaking about grief. It has been a constant in my life and a pathway to authentic connection with others. It has been a common denominator, like birth.

We all die. Every loss contains some sorrow and consumes us for a time. The stages of grief are more like a jumble of questions, especially when death arrives in complicated situations. Why does anyone die young? Or painfully, or before family arrives, or without resolution, or in any incomprehensible way? And then grief becomes the ongoing experience of living with loss, living into loss, living beyond loss. Anderson Cooper's podcast *That's All There Is* demonstrates again and again how so many of us experiencing tragic loss climb up to breathe the air again, knowing we will succumb occasionally to dwell in that deep place of grief. And we will also return to the fresh air and find memories, sounds, and smells that wrap us with love, reminding us that our loved one lives on in us and holds us. We find ways to take them with us into our singular future life.

*A time to weep, and a time to laugh;
a time to mourn, and a time to dance*
—Ecclesiastes 3:4 KJV

About the Author

Maeve A. Cullinane started writing poetry as a young girl, and never stopped. Her prose and fiction are better for it. After graduate school, she taught writing as an elementary school teacher, was a blogger for the local newspaper, and is currently working on a novel. She has attended and facilitated grief workshops and support groups, participated in the National Alliance on Mental Illness' Family to Family program, and incorporates mindfulness and meditation practices into her daily life. She lives with her dog, Charlie, and loves her three adult children and their partners who are spread across the Northeast. Connect with Maeve on Substack @maevecullinaneauthor and on Instagram @maevec.author.